THE CREDIT

THE CREDIT

A COMEDY OF EMPEIRIA[1]
IN THREE ACTS

AUGUSTUS YOUNG

All rights reserved. No part of this work covered by the copyright herein may be reproduced or used in any means – graphic, electronic, or mechanical, including copying, recording, taping, or information storage and retrieval systems – without written permission of the publisher.

Printed by imprintdigital
Upton Pyne, Exeter
www.digital.imprint.co.uk

Typesetting and cover design by narrator
www.narrator.me.uk
info@narrator.me.uk
033 022 300 39

First edition published by Menard/Advent Press in 1980/1986
www.menardpress.co.uk

© Augustus Young

Revised second edition published in 2018
Ireland: The Duras Press ISBN 978-0-9568379-9-8
UK: Menard Press 978-1-874320-71-5

© Drawings by John Parsons
© Cover photo by Jez Timms on Unsplash

The moral right of the author has been asserted.

A nod to Ed Dorn and a wink to Brian Coffey

CONTENTS

ACT ONE (p. 1)

20th June

Brother Jim, the narrator, retired from secular life to become a janitor and sacristan in a Jesuit school, recounts the return of the ultimate conformist pupil, Hugo, now a bean factory owner in Italy. The event is overshadowed by the uninvited presence of a certain Doc McGuiness, possibly his business partner. Head teacher pontificates, and Hugo says what is expected. As an envoi, Brother Jim consider the formation of human beings, with the emphasis on speech development. And places Suck and other ex-students in their world, and ponders Hugo and success in life, and sees both as a projection.

ACT TWO (p. 39)

8th July

Hugo's death is reported from Venice by Doc McGuiness. A Requiem Mass is celebrated in his hometown. Doc books into Hotel Chi, Chioggia where he drinks himself into the stupor and is haunted by bad dreams.

9th July

Conflicting accounts of Hugo's death.
An 'eye-witness' describes his disappearance from a vaporetto. A human leg is recovered from the lagoon. Fleur joins Doc in Hotel Chi.

ACT THREE (p. 70)

10th July

Two black students, Vector and Velocity, while exploring the sewers of Cioccolato, a hill-town, spot a body in an underground factory. Sitting at the feet of a living statue of Dante Alighieri, they exchange pre-rap patter and white substances with him. Fleur and Doc arrive in Cioccolato and meet Vector and Velocity while posing as tourists. Dante takes them on a guided tour of the lower depths of the town, and they end up in the bean factory, where they find Hugo's body half-buried, but showing signs of life. As they dig him out, an earthquake hits Cioccolato.

Act One

CANTO ONE

First let me introduce myself
I'm Brother James (priests call me Jim).
Of married love and modest wealth
I've had my fill, and now I'm in
a teaching order for my health.
It's better than a loony bin.
At least I'm certain who I am:
School Janitor and Sacristan.

An oddsbody for twenty years,
the scourge of little boys, I haunt
the doubtful places where the dears
monkey to men, and leave buoyant,
ready to reckon with careers,
women and cancers. My vantage point
that of a speck, but on the spot;
mutatis mutandis, I've seen the lot.

And sleep comes hard: My mind is packed
with cheeky brats become great brutes;
like screaming grasshoppers that hack
 the shrinking, shrieking mandrake roots.
My former charges now attack
and chop me up with billyhooks.
So, boiled in sputum, I'm a stew
for midnight feasts dreamed up by Hugh.

CANTO TWO

This Hugo was a credit to
the Christian Brothers and the Nuns,
straightforward educators who
made mothers proud of manly sons.
Though sometimes beaten black and blue
to teach him manners and his sums,
Hugh learned to like them; they imbued
in him a healthy attitude.

Thus inroads on the beast were made.
 The youngster came to hold his own
with fluffy buns and lemonade
in anybody's drawing room.
Practiced in the tricks of the trade
to please his betters, soon Hugh'd grown
wised up enough in worldly ways
to make his life an act of faith.

Faith did not blind. Hugh saw to it,
caught in the act, to catch the mood
of those who made a law of it,
and took the blame, and always stood
humbly by while elders jawed it.
A tear or two, all to the good.
He had received a thorough grooming
from his mentors in being human.

His best side shown, Hugh faced the stick,
a paragon of stoic poise;
and while the strokes came thin and thick,
he numbed himself and made no noise,
nonchalant (though cut to the quick);
but this won whistles from the boys,
and new life from the flagging cane
to brand Hugh with collective blame.

Though Hugh's report sure ruin spelt, SP
the family did not despair.
The father thought it rich, what wealth!
and hummed a long forgotten air:
'At Your Age No Better Myself'.
The women signed, and said a prayer.
'To Have Been Caught Is A Good Sign,
But You'll Meet Your Match The Next Time'

Which came to pass: the beloved son
was put into my Jesuit school,
an all-in place second to none
for ragamuffin renewal.
At first lost, he used his gumption,
and on misfortune did not drool.
He learned the notice board off pat,
and found a natural habitat.

The ruling passion, new boy nosed,
was Bringing Out The Best. Discreet,
the priests were tolerant of those
who hid their worst side underneath;
well aware that *comme il faut* is
a camouflage for the complete
young man to fashion a career in
a world where there's no second hearing.

I watched this mere boy take the hint.
Who dropped it? Not the marble saint
perched at the entrance on a plinth
bedded in ivy; when it rained
a choice cover for wunderkind…
Hugo one wet day made his name:
'He climbed The Statue of Loyola,
Baptising it in Coca-Cola'.

My picture of Hugh will not fade.
It's mental. How can I forget
an average boy who often played
typical tricks, and was no pet;
who with beatings only, obeyed
the rule of thumb, until a *bète
noire* for bruises made him adroit
in the true art of not being caught.

Hugh, trainee toff, wore, like a kilt,
a blazer almost to his knees;
a collar smudged with finger filth;
and flannel pants with a sharp crease;
his schoolboy cap, worn at a tilt,
was doffed to masters with due ease,
despite a most unruly quiff.
His style, though odd, wasn't obtrusive.

Obtrusion was a game he played
with lesser mortals of his own
age and station (though hamper raids
called for due caution). When at home
he might disgrace himself with maids,
but left his sisters' friends alone.
His stealth approaching loose loose change,
or Christmas cake, was windlike, strange,

Returned to school, he learned to duck
distasteful tasks. Tricks didn't fail
if a balanced bargain was struck:
one couldn't call it black blackmail;
for instance, finding a friend tuck
into another's parcel mail,
one either shared it like a pig,
or bartered silence for a crib.

Now Hugh was seen to be whole hog
behind school spirit, manifest
in smoking butt ends in the bog,
and bellowing school songs with zest.
Though joining in was a hard slog
to begin with, being like the rest
made sense whenever trouble brewed;
one's covered by the multitude.

Though none too brave, and the wrong build
for contact sports, he made the team
as second sub; no natural skill
did not discount the lad from being
on the ball when the whistle stilled
play, and the trainer spied his clean
break, though spoiled by a foul. This meant
for travel games he always went.

What's more, although he couldn't sing,
school operas always need a man;
and letting himself be roped in,
he opened his mouth, and never sang.
No harm done to his reputation:
parents and sisters with priests cram
the hallowed hall, and he looked great
holding the boards as a pirate.

All-rounder! All one wants to be.
School success is not specific;
a golden mean to baulk envy;
and sisters thought him terrific.
Parents were gratified to see
Hugh settle down and scrape his Matric.
The Church, they hoped; but SJs saw
a future here in Criminal Law

Hugh's leaving was a little death.
It always is: the vacant place
in chapel, class and where he ate,
filled with imposters, a disgrace:
Compared with last year's lot they're wet,
slightly deformed and clearly base.
School life goes on. Some years he's quit.
His memory has become a myth.

CANTO THREE

Once out of school most boys go free,
and only return in bad dreams.
There are a few that frighteningly
boomerang back, recessive genes,
as teachers. All they wish to be!
In truth, the very thought blasphemes,
as though the afterlife were nothing
more spirited than return rutting'.

Some more slink back in dribs and drabs,
the outside world getting too much;
jejune jobs and married to nags,
worrying about the future and such.
Through memories, mainly ersatz,
they tap the past, and get in touch
with mellower masters, who invite
the prodigals to P.P. night:

reunions run by former Sucks,
who floated into cushy jobs;
full members of the school Ku Klux.
Now bloated like successful frogs,
they leap through life, and life's de-luxe,
devoted to their breeding bogs.
Of course School hogs them as envoys,
to raise funds and round up Old Boys

for get-togethers—pints and pies
in private bars (no ladies please);
the stranglehold of old school ties,
and buttoned blazers, a tight squeeze.
Banter abounds, but no cheap jibes.
The past's the present. It would please
their dead parents: such healthy fun,
crowding round some old school album.

Men will be boys, scrouch down to scan,
with shirt tails out, school photographs.
The past self's seen as a hard man,
and classmates as a load of laughs.
Street meetings would have made them clam
(who wants to play have-nots and haves);
but they can face an early version.
(It surely was another person.)

Hugh's year was useless at this stag
commemoration cum carouse.
The Suck in charge felt interest flag.
(This crowd is flaccid as dry cows.)
He took a Yearbook from his bag,
opened it for a corporate browse
at their class group. 'Where are they now?'
was written on his raised eyebrow.

The Old Boys bucked up as they scoured
the pictures like a repaid debt.
No detail was to be ignored.
A life, at one remove, to fete.
Yet their high spirits soon lowered,
lighting on the lunette inset
with Hugh in it, to Cheshire cat
over the faithful who just sat.

This proved too much. All comers threw
themselves into the creamy pints;
with 'early night tonight', withdrew,
withholding what was on their minds:
'The class group travesty is true.
We are a bunch of left behinds
compared to…' Who? The Boys despair:
'How can we breathe? Hugh fills the air.'

Suck held the photo to the light.
Trust Hugh to be the only one
not there when taken; only right
trick camera work had to be done.
He's orbed above the sitting tight
nonentities, man in the sun,
a none-too-human spot-the-ball;
good reason for their jealous gall.

'Past pupil photo of the year,
pride of place in the school brochure,
Hugo's head and shoulders appear
bubbling above massed classmates who're
nondescript beside their compeer,
whose driving power as a doer
stands out. No college boy, one can tell:
His Own Business and Doing Well.

'Hugh's entry, though, is non-committal,
name and initials, nothing else;
no cod degree, like the despicable
B.A. (Econ.), to boost himself.
His mystique remains a riddle
that's answered only by a wealth
of speculation of the kind
a real success need never mind.

'For instance, say, that sidelong look
and careful parting; these can't hide
the bald patch that is a textbook
tonsure, denoting a brutal side.
The angle that the camera took,
his best profile, makes him one eyed,
which must reflect the cyclopean
thunderbolts he holds for women.

'Which means he has an iceberg eye
for hot pieces with names like Letty,
whose scheme would be to suck him dry
at 'Dante Gabriel Rossetti',
a bistro where they'd meet the high
and mighty, eligible for confetti
once the latest divorce comes through;
the next one starts, old wives for new.

'He's down to earth in his conduct,
and never known to misbehave
with a *femme seul* of usufruct,
unless an understanding's made
that his terms of amorous truck
are strictly business. So well paid
escorts (*noli me tàngere* types)
are seen with him on gala nights.

'This only to divert the Press.
His friends and colleagues know those chic
chaperones in Saragasso dress
are the standard blondes of a slick
dating deal, not flames in the flesh,
who come to make the cameras click;
medusas on the premier rung
of showbiz; not gotterdammerung.

'The finger underneath his chin
is reassuring, a sure sign
that careless living's not for him; .
a family man, given time;
on it he wears a grandma's ring
for somebody's daughter who's condign;
the wife he patents in his dreams,
a pretty miss with private means.

'A finishing school in Switzerland,
she waits for him, and the first kiss;
her dowry to the lucky husband
whose prospects are as pa would wish;
and daddy is a public servant,
and dutiful too his daughter is;
brought up of course not to mention
money, but knowing he's her pension.

'Maybe they'll meet in the foyer
of, say, a bank in St Moritz.
But there we have another story
many a bag of fish and chips
will be wrapped in; still, it bores me,
putting together the juicy bits…
for a story worked up in toto
from (Suck sneered) a touched-up photo.

'Success in life. What can that be?
In simpler times the weaker sex,
then women, strong on security,
would tell you. Now the question's vexed.
The answer's not posterity;
who could wait that long for prospects?
Suck put shillyshallying aside:
It's something for failures to decide.

CANTO FOUR

A chance news item from Siam.
Such spotted it. Through Reuter fog
the picture peered, more diagram
than photo, pointillistic log
of what might be a business man
shaking hands with a Mekong mob,
background monsoon… the legend, yes,
confounds the school scout: Hugh, no less.

Ex-boy made good. Suck found his brief
and took the cutting to the Head.
Head pondered it. 'Beyond belief,
that's Hugh. I thought that he was dead…
Some business trip… Oxfam relief…
Feared lost. No! That was Norman, Ned,
or was it Crean? I'm pleased Hugh's living;
get him present at Prize-giving.

'We need as usual to impress.
But not too much. I will of course
prepare his speech. Last year's address,
yours, I'm afraid, was quite off course.
An eagerness led to excess.
(In less I find there is more force.)
But back to Hugh… around his mouth
there's something powerful; dig him out.

'But see the Committee just in case
there's something we don't know about.
I haven't met him face to face
since O so long. Still I would doubt
from this portrait that he'd disgrace
the school. But vet him inside out,
and outside in, with all due care.
Our catchment parents will be there.'

Committees: who doesn't deplore them,
going through the motions. Nothing new;
the chairman, waiting for a quorum,
co-opts himself; he counts as two.
Who seconds that? The four of them
shoot up their hands. So six set to
a dodo race of bored bombast.
Suck held Head's question to the last.

And weary, wanting to get home,
the committee couldn't care less.
Hugo's profile, hurriedly shown,
is judged ' the dead spit of success';
and 'after all, he's one of our own';
'well worth his place'; and 'who'd have guessed'.
The members as a body rise,
the next date fixed for alibis.

Suck stayed to draft a studied note.
'Dear Head, your feelings were confirmed.
It didn't even go to a vote.
All above board. No gossip learned
of albatrosses round his throat.
A reputation quietly earned,
low key enough to be controlled.
A credit to the school, all told.'

Head read and sighed. A young tycoon
and no upstart. He had a feel
for money mystics who're in tune
with higher things than a quick deal.
And conjuring up the Church in ruin,
saw Hugo crack the Seventh Seal
with a neon cross and a sixth sense:
a cash crusade like Peter's Pence.

Head shook himself. 'In my old age
such dated dreams! This Hugh must be
a rerum² boss whose workers' wage
is just. (Pope Leo's man, like me.)
Left wing at heart… Stock market played
only to boost some charity.
His bounty there, with income tax
deducted, no fiscal virtue lacks.'

Head's thoughts go to the Building Fund.
'Our jumble sales, whist drives, flag days
and dinner dances, don't expunge
the interest on the loan we've raised.
Our cash campaign is moribund.
All donkey work, we bank the brays.
A big time begging, by telex,
is wanted, and some blanket cheques.

'Dear Suck, don't hesitate to ask
your man. He'll do.' The hide and seek
of verse can't catch the cordial bask
of easy prose in Pauline pique.
Verbatim, it would only mask
a message that was not oblique.
'School headed paper', 'Surnames', 'Sign
pp. for me' and 'Send on time'.

Hugh got Suck's note while in Bangkok,
where he was selling off a plant.
The letter was a knock for knock.
The ripe request gave Hugh his hand.
He showed it to his client, Doc
McGuinness, who grew sycophant.
'I'll sign straight off.' Hugh thought of school.
'It comes in handy. What a fool.'

'Dear Suck.' Hugh's letter was succinct.
His secretary would spell it out
in office prose, until it linked.
'Head's billing letter made me proud.
Do let him know I'm tickled pink.
Can't wait to coo that catchment crowd.
A formal 'Yes' will follow this.
Nothing to lose. My person's his.'

CANTO FIVE

Life starts—egged on by needy seed—
when the genomes are put in place
by a lottery which will breed
what makes a slave or master race.
The luck of the draw is the decreed
mix of the grandparent's gene base.
Freaks lead to feuds. Whose side's at fault?
Gorge rises in the family vault.

Genetics is a game that plays
in nurseries. The copy cat
in children in their early days
mimics monkeys, sicut erat…
Still the aping of ancestral ways
in adult life can only fall flat.
No one's born a fait accompli
as preordained by Mendel's pea.

What's handed on is handed out
by parents' and teachers' so say.
Thus, heredity we flout.
The future's nurture, come what may.
Lamarck's the name to bandy about.
He'll make the natural law obey.
The best deceived plump for the trope,
you're what you make yourself. There's hope.

Hugh baulks at that. We're ready-made.
And can rise above Environment—
the swaddling clothes in which we're laid
on the world's scales for the parent
to mold us into a fit state
for life. But he has to relent:
orphaning yourself by parricide
would be Nurture. The idea died.

Still the dregs of mother's milk can
remain to haunt the weaned off-spring,
regurgitating in the grown man.
Pavlovian bells his feed time ring.
This happens when life lacks élan.
And he returns to his origins
to bemoan the heirloom ill-spent,
and be absolved by a parent.

Hugh wasn't exempt from the claims
of generators, pro and con.
Parents had him, he had them; pains
stubbornly shared; suffering's son
who grew from playpens to tight reins,
to be broke into right and wrong
by bribes and blackmail and 'no sweets,
unless you're good'. Hugh was, for treats.

Suck had his line in Jesuit jokes
and wrote to Hugo's parents. They
were most surprised. Was it a hoax?
The letter heading read S.J…
But they accepted like good folks,
regretting it the very next day:
'If Hugh wanted us…' (Such scruples
are quite unknown among marsupials.)

CANTO SIX

At best our memories are myths,
the persons in them better dead.
So the past and present are quits,
giving them a future instead.
So the recapitulation fits.
No backward look to tempt regret.
What's true or false are absolutes,
beyond distinction when it suits.

Cloud cuckoo land has not a cloud.
Why should it—not a whit to hide.
The cuckoo's coo rings clear and loud:
Immortals only have a best side,
demons are angels. All's allowed
in retrospect. One's gratified.
Unless a well-known figure from
the past comes back, it goes ding-dong.

On Hugh's return, the myth made man
was chauffeured in at twelve o'clock.
A second birth! Although his mam
was not aware what she had dropped
on the fresh-laid tarmacadam
of the alma mater where he'd rocked
from fame to fortune. Ring the bell:
delivered safe, and doing well.

The pupils flocked around the Rolls,
and scattered smart when Head appeared
Some scrouched behind the grassy knolls
that fringed the mud of playing fields.
A brave few saw (all seeing moles)
Hugh lose his footing, as he reeled
out of de-luxe-dom to wet land.
Then straighten himself to meet Head's hand.

All heroes need the human touch.
Head was relieved, and blessed his luck.
Hugh had the handshake of a Dutch
rotary chairman, not like Suck.
His savoir faire (and foul) was much
 more apparent in close truck:
the aura of almighty trust
one swoons to in the upper crust.

The Old Boys took a cagier view,
The legend and the legerdemain
was after all only their Hugh.
Still, who'd have banked on real champagne
(Hugh had it sent, and seed cake, too).
The luncheon party didn't complain,
accustomed to a midday stout
gave Hugh the benefit of the doubt.

The Governors arrived too late
to savor this refreshing touch.
These dignitaries usually rate
such little doos as less than much.
And most; having enough on their plate,
excuse themselves and send on fudge,
or whatever's their latest line.
The keen ones drop in and short time.

One was a dentist, a sly sponge,
who put a drop of alcohol
on patients' nostrils to expunge
his boozy breath. Hugh used sol
volatile vines. The champers plunged
his guests into a moral hol,
and toasts lit up the atmosphere.
Headboy alone could smell things clear,

being young, with each olfactory bud
in primavera, to him the stink
would knock grown men down with a thud
to pave the floor like an ice rink
where guests revolved, for Head-boy's blood
was up and alive, he smelt distinct
a vapour, vodka. Could it be
someone had spiked Hugh's Russian tea?

Still Hugo stood as on a cloud,
composed, upright (sculptors take note).
Around his pedestal the crowd
weaved webs of wonder, and it clothes
the mystery with a cloak or shroud
(depending on which way's bespoke),
a blank wall, or a concrete sphinx
 whose secret's only what one thinks.

Suck watched the window, as convoys
of parents cluttered up the drive,
and were picked out by nervous boys
who ran to stop them hooting. 'I've
noticed the brutes abhor the noise
progenitors make when they arrive,
and with dumb play would have them know…'
Suck thought dark thoughts (too dark to show).

Hugh's parents, it's of interest, made
it by taxi. The moving scene
between them and their son forbade
too close a look. But having seen
too many prodigals cascade,
with borrowed charms, the old blood stream,
to mistake the formal correct
in Hugh for what you would expect…

They met with Head and Suck on flank.
The guests before them, every eye—
one Governor, six Old Boys, swank
gate crashing parents—wiped (though dry);
except Head-boy who looked on blank.
All three wished the other two'd die.
Still facts were met, and it went fine,
despite ten years since the last time.

Restraint lent dignity. Of course
sang froid seemed natural. Families
can do without the gushy source
which floods when love's not at its ease.
By holding back it finds its force.
The dam banks on being hard to please.
Still sparks in crisis. Thus Hugh's palm
met dad's, his cheek was brushed by mam.

The party moved into the hall.
The uproar shut off. In conclave,
pupils and parents, feeling small,
almost stood up. To misbehave
brings them closer together. They spoil
to rebel and be really brave.
The chaos of chitchat resumed,
louder, of course. Head, smiling, fumed.

Or did he? On an open day
when goodwill's at a premium,
as parents to their proxies pay
homage, and see how school is run,
all discipline that's on display's
fair target for some modest fun.
And Head relaxed but on his guard
(term time reflexes do die hard).

He took a breath. The status quo's
assured. Through stain-glass windows shafts
of sunlight split the catchment rows
to carry dust in golden wafts.
He saw glass cases that enclose
books to the roof, and the riff-raff
walled in by bound volumes of what
must be stood by, *Dieu et Mon Droit*,

transfigured briefly in his mind
(a library that had no place
for human interest of the kind
that has no future left to face,
such as in novels that will wind
up all lifetimes on the last page),
a vision of what was to come,
as though it were all past and done.

And Head saw Hugh, Old Boy of Note,
do the school proud with a speech, short
and to the point, each chosen quote
pronounced with brio and with heart
enough to make the parents gloat
and afterwards declare it art
with a large A, a private word
made public for the chosen herd.

Still, Hugh's speech was still to come.
Head's text was trimmed so it would be
exactly as every other one
since school began, nothing left free,
despite the fact that Hugh was someone
('spoken for by being asked by me').
Still, some things can't be given as read
from a name that's not household yet.

CANTO SEVEN

One unexpected guest was there.
A panama topped the front row,
crowning a suit in true mohair,
Cellini pin on polka dot bow;
a bolstered beacon, point blank stare,
cherubic cheeks in full flambeau.
It's Doc McGuiness from Bangkok.
The platform mounts the stage en bloc.

There Head and Suck and Hugh were joined
by teachers too tired to escape.
With thunderclapping duly doyened,
Head raised a finger to the gape
of phalanxed parents, and he fawned,
'Allow me a word.' The outbreak
like lightning lulled: a soloist
coming in to cadenza Liszt!

Head's speech was spiced with epigram,
weighed words that scream to be together
when crowded into stanzas cram-
full of wisdom, wit, whatever,
cadged from Baltasar Gracian,[3]
a Jesuit, more of the letter
than the spirit, a *homme de coeur*
for sacerdotes and Schopenhauer.

Head spoke of KNOWLEDGE, gained from books;
EXPERIENCE, from our fellow men;
and HOLY WISDOM, when one looks
to oneself to find peace, amen.
'THE TRUTH needs tact, world's full of crooks;
and REAL BELIEF'S the exception.
THE ART OF LIVING's to know where,
and when, and how, to sell fresh air;

'and don't espouse the first account
you hear, and treat as concubines
subsequent versions. The SOUND
CHOICE comes by waiting for star signs
with your feet firmly on the ground;
great good sense, along the lines
A DAY WITHOUT A QUARREL means
A good night's sleep and pleasant dreams.

'Though stubbornness is a tumour,
the monstrous daughter of passion,
being TOO FREE is fatal. HUMOUR
is only rational in ration.
Bound by RULES one can do no more
than recherche slaves of fashion.
AVOID INSULTS: it saves revenge.
By CHOICE, NOT CHANCE, DECIDE YOUR FRIENDS.

'COMPASSION: one should always strive
to help the down. But don't malign
the *creme de crème*. Those who thrive.
No cause to make success a crime.'
And more, 'THE LOGOS'S last to arrive,
limping along on the arm of TIME.'
And so on... Head's wiseacres were
stunning; so heard without a stir.

He looked around. The crowd came to.
His eyes on Hugh act as their guide.
'Each year we get a proud son who
has made his name in the world outside
to speak seven minutes to you,
and present top pupils a prize.
This day, high commerce's lent us one.
He doesn't need an introduction.'

Hugh got on feet (with stealth, to deal
with vertigo—he hadn't dined).
Once vertical, how did he feel:
before him, all he'd left behind.
Emotion, no. His eyes pre-spiel
searched for a stooge face to spellbind.
In the front row one caught his eye.
He paused. Close readers will guess why.

Hugh paused, a pause perpetuated
by hallfulls of bated breath
ready to swallow what's prated.
He paused too long, and Head broke sweat.
Grand apnoeas were created,
the air was pawed till lungs were let
in sepulchral sighs, like second wind
from a dead body. The silence sinned.

Doc suddenly slid back his seat
which creaked out as it scraped the floor,
and with a loud yawn raised his feet.
Hugh watched for worse. Doc did no more
than get up, tip-toe out, a feat
observed by all, and slammed the door.
Dead silence in the hall went bang.
Hugo's delivery began:

'Boys, reverend fathers, gentlemen,
(mustn't forget the ladies too)
I'm taken aback, and back to when
I came among you first, a new
little fellow whose fountain pen
leaked in his pocket, and with few
friends to speak of. I say with pride,
you're all colleagues now, tested and tried…'

Suffice to say, Hugh's speech was dull.
It had to be. Head boy was rapt
with reason, if he guessed the gull.
Hugh read Head's précis, word exact,
but at a speed that made it null
and void, a ventriloquist's act.
And dummied through, it more than did
to please the parents. Obsequies rid,

Hugh soon was lost among the guests,
gathering round, drawing devout
attention to themselves as conquests.
His smile and handshake made them proud.
Mid rivaling parties, and pests
with visiting cards, he slipped out
unnoticed as the host ranks closed
about his more gregarious ghost…

and wasn't missed. The pouncing throng
were glued together in a jam
that bottlenecked them to belong
to each other. And no one can
move, except in a mass along
the aisle, a congregated 'I am',
not personal; united folk
in a curdling kaleidoscope.

Who shakes it? Not Head, Suck or Hugh.
To make it flow you'd need to be
the wizard of the cosmic cue,
a four dimension trinity.
A fast-forward will have to do:
parents meet parents, once they're free,
by mutual sons mutually sized,
and as somebodies recognized.

It's common knowledge that Head received
a missive that was franked freepost
next day, and opened it, and heaved
a sigh of thanks. It was the lowest
big cheque that could have been believed
as more than less, though more than most:
the covering letter must have been lost;
signed 'Hugo' (sic). It was uncrossed.

CANTO EIGHT

Our precursors from ape ages
named things wrongly to begin with
—dead expression on flat faces:
—tongue out to the utter limit:
—knew no better. Commonplaces
good enough for homo dimwit,
patented to improvise on
contradictions, and build lies on.

Babel's Tower was not demolished.
The toppled folly, being prefab,
sprung up, sideways: pretty, polished
portacabins, a language lab
for every tongue to evolve wished
word-walhallas in global gab[4],
cosmic converse which never stops
to think that talk's all malaprops.[5]

Which brings me back to Suck and Co.,
boys young and Old, the parents too,
protagonists these verses throw
together, Head and Doc and Hugh.
In benediction or mal mot?
Theodicy I won't pursue,
semantics, or what's other than
my sacred call as sacristan.

As janitor my job needs brains,
with fifty heads for schoolboy schemes.
I'm Cerberus to what profanes
school life and death, source of bad dreams.
But caught off guard by orphic strains
sleep shanghais me, and mental means
are not enough as all hell breaks
loose, in fifty minds and headaches.

As sacristan or holy fool,
in the vestiary at first light,
my *raison d'etre* is ritual.
The altar's laid, the candles light.
I am the Brahmin of the school
who charons souls across the night.
My bells will bring the whole world here.
I genuflect and disappear.

Who comes? Head first, a spry priest grown
accustomed to early birds and worms,
talking to himself, testing tone,
putting day's brief on friendly terms
with breviaries and what's best known
for peace sake or goodly returns.
In short, the bon ton of 'Let's pass
doubt to the doubter, and say Mass'.

A young Suck follows in Head's wake.
He serves to serve, but with a smirk
obvious as a Scot on the make
(on his way to Chapel not Kirk),
not certain whether to overtake
and salute Head, and claim a perk
as early riser number one.
The prospect makes him want to run.

Next, young Old Boys, sleep besotted,
straggle behind, like slug-worms will
in a trail, not to be spotted.
Instinct tells them, could be trouble,
Bedraggled, ties and hair half knotted,
bunching wary in a bubble,
horns withdrawn to blunt pricks, slob sure,
their outlook on the world's obscure.

Where's Hugo? Not in this parade
Our sleeping hero scorns to be
disturbed mid-dream. In bed he stayed.
The silence in the dormitory
is poetry I can't create.
Still, after breakfast he'll face me,
and I'll strop upon his person,
not an event to write verse on.

Meanwhile, my better part must bless
his sanctuary. In profound sleep
the creature finds his own Loch Ness
to surface from, but dreams still keep
their secret, leaving others to guess
what can't be fathomed, being too deep:
the images that are in him
far from my powers to imagine.

Success in life is beyond me.
I bow before the great unknowns
telescoped in their tondi
each sits on a telluric throne.
More Paul Veronese than Paul Klee.
More Milton than some patchwork poem.
Wonders of the world, not one day,
transfiguring the anima mundi.

BROTHER JIM'S ENVOI

Before conception, we're reptile
replicas of each other. Birth
makes no difference. Hospital-file
mix-ups mean nothing, no one's hurt.
The changelings have the self-same smile,
and smell, and glaxo-growing girth;
identikit blobs, until the urge
to grasp what's what makes us diverge.

The quest for knowing brings unique
reflexes into play. We crawl
creatively, eat earth, and speak
in tongues, not Chomsky's patois, bawl
out the shibboleths of pure cheek.
The plosives aren't patterned at all
by tribal promptings, nascent noise
broadcasting corybantic joys.

All vowels out (in Vico's view,
one for each sense, quinti-passion),
we raise a vocal curlicue
free floating in diapason,
sesquipedalian… cou-cou
interrupts so we can pass on
to high pitched hoots, that don't suggest
we're cuckoos burdening the nest

but wise young owls who listen long
and hard before speaking. Then crank
out from the blueprint primal song,
live poetry, and not the *manqué*
immortal kind which has a strong
death wish, belshazzaring what's blank
with riddles; more a *terre-a-terre*
rejoicing like 'Kilroy Was Here'.

The infant oracle's 'Baa waah'
heralds the piping of a bird
and ma hears 'ma', and da 'da da'
They catch the holophrastic word
that means so much to them. 'Ga ga'.
The chant goes on but isn't heard
So the baby keeps its breath in.
A pietas is in possession.

All parents fall for this mistake.
These utterings of utter chance
are chordal courants (oral Blake
"Flame Delights In Its Form"), larynx,
dancing up and down for its own sake,
deaf to the world, without consonants,
well-being being given its free voice
(so science says to annoy us).

Perpetual sound from the voice box—
a putti trick! Mere neonates
get short of wind. A paradox:
air is stopped, not to suffocate.
And crowing like congested cocks
the stop-gap fricatives castrate
blubbering vowels, and give vent
to the first morphemes, and fall silent.

We breathe again. A pleural pinch.
And babbles, ten to the breath, grow
organised (only the goldfinch
notates in bars its prime say-so).
But as to meaning we don't flinch,
being to ourselves the only show,
one not too wild, and on parole,
the counts-to-ten mean self-control.[6]

Beyond a chaos of child care
provides a ready-made cocoon
that fits us like new baby wear,
a world we outgrew like the womb.
Where once a breast was brought to bare,
some saps are offered on a spoon,
crammed down the throat. What's really changed
goes deeper than being toilet trained.

Our two begetters are driven
to re-enact survival scenes.
Then social decrees are given,
in order's name, to curb extremes.
Darwin got it right, to fit in,
mothers black-breast unwilling weans.
Paternal dictates like tut-tut
pot-bind us, independence cut.

Forced to depend on paddy-cries,
rhubarbarians around us swarm,
organic paeans cut down to size,
and so the mother tongue is born.
Our language acquisition device
(or L.A.D.) begins to form
in phrases from consensus glotts,
to patterpult like Pope's parrots.

This soundpost reached, soliloquies
become what others want to hear:
backchat, that is, gregarious glees,
full of quotations like Shakespeare.
The ethnocentric telegraphese
gains grammar, and the general ear,
and with it the wordly sentence.
So the pure ego era ends.

Our soloings were, so to speak,
throwbacks to primal pantomime,
when bodying forth the whole physique
took the tongue's part, and gave it spine.
Shot-putter grunts expressed the peak
of synergy, The World Is Mine.
With feet enough to fall back on,
quadrupals could dance a chaconne.

Bipeds, like you and me, cannot.
Not even a passepied. It takes two
to keep upright, a pas-de-twot

(figure that out)[7]. Most must make do
with mouth-mimes, one might call voxtrot.
Stands in good stead a Head or Hugh
who watch their footings and hold forth,
concords of sweet nothings outpoured.

NOTES: ACT ONE

[1] 'In conversation some time ago, Goethe had remarked that Byron had too much empeiria. I did not well understand what he meant; but I forbore to ask, and thought of the matter in silence. However, I got nothing by reflection, and found I must wait till my improved culture or some happy circumstance should unlock the secret....' (Eckermann, *Conversations with Goethe*).

[2] *Rerum Novarum*: papal encyclical defining duties of employers to workers (Leo XIII, 1891).

[3] Baltasar Gracian (1601–1658), Spanish Jesuit, diplomat and author. Works include *Manual y Arte de Prudencia* (*The Oracle, a Manual of the Art of Discretion*).

[4] 'We must imagine early language as consisting of very long words full of difficult sounds, and sung rather than spoken. Once all speech was something between the nightly love lyrics of puss on the tiles and the melodious love songs of the nightingale... these long conglomerations of sounds... strings of syllables... articulated into language through the tendency to shorten the word-chant in order to make pronunciation more easy. Difficult combinations of sounds are discarded, those only being retained which are easy to pronounce' (O. Jespersen, *Language, Its Nature, Development and Origin*, 1964).

'Originally man expressed his ideas by gesture, but as he gesticulated with his hands, his tongue, lips and jaw unconsciously followed in a ridiculous fashion, "understudying" the actions of the hands. The consequence was that when, owing to pressure of other business, the principal actors (the hands) retired from the stage—as much as principal actors ever do—their understudies, the tongue, lips and jaw, were already proficient in the pantomimic art. Then the great discovery was made that if while making a gesture with the tongue and lips, air was blown through the nasal or oral cavities, the gesture became audible...' (Sir Richard Paget, *Human Speech*, 1930).

'Speaking out loud when alone is imprudent. It establishes thought on such friendly terms with speech that the gulf between what we say and feel is narrowed. A bad habit...' (Schopenhauer).

'The fault with our books and other deeds is that they are too human. I want something speaking in some means to the condition of muskrats and the skunk cabbages'... (Thoreau).

5 Parmenides (fifth century BC) thought that originally names had been given to things on the basis of 'wrong thinking' and that the continued use of the original names perpetuated the errors of men's earlier thinking about the objects around them.

6 Counts to ten: birds and mammals cannot learn to 'count' beyond eight; ten is the average interval for a breathless infant to recover from the consonant stop in order to vowel again.

7 *Theological Wordbook of the Old Testament*, edited Harris et al., or *The Art of Tango*, Carlos Gardel.

Act Two

"The discovery
we exist
was man's fall".

– R. W. Emerson

CANTO NINE

> "Quod licet Jovi, non licet bovi"
> – Anon

What's death between coeval friends?
A cause for pause and angst audit;
the shocking news belief suspends.
The live ones learn to live with it:
death brings to mind what fate portends
for everyone, the same exit,
the self included, we're all dying.
It thrills to have escaped this time.

Hugh's sudden death thrilled quite a few.
Cathedrals of sepulchral folk
in his hometown paid homage to
a famous son when the news broke.
Still would his requiem have filled a pew—
the known facts being a pig-in-the-poke—
if Hugh's last lesson had been read
from the point of view of the dead?

Who cares? The term 'untimely's heard
'So young' (at forty); 'Who could tell';
'The end of an era' is murmured.
Enough to make the body smell.
The public exit-pot is stirred;
ingredients begin to gel
(Saints don't corrupt being salted lamb.
Could this legume be *foule medame*?)

A sudden death at forty-one
could not be cerebral of course;
a coronary in one so young
wouldn't have had the heart to thrombose;
no accident—his luck would run;
foul-play might fake an overdose.
But Doc McGuiness disclosed, 'Hugh
at last check up was subject to

>   advanced enlargement of the brain,
>   restriction of the scrotum, gas,
>   pineal gland failure, groin strain
>   stones in the urine that won't pass.
>   All aggravated by Wagnerian
>   pudenda pulped to a goulash
>   by a too tight truss'. And so on.
>   Hugh's health by all accounts was gone.

The question everyone's asking:
what was Hugh doing in Venice in July?

Not Harry's Bar or the Lido,
the Excelsior, or the Gritti, but
on a crowded vaporetto

a stone-throw
from the ghetto;

at the time of the year,
the time of the day,
when the oldest sewer in the world meets the sky.

We doubt his business was to die;
at the time of the day,
the time of the year

when the sun is a veiled beast behind
the bars of an electric storm,
and the unknown tourist wishes he hadn't been born.

We doubt his business was to die. He had better things to do.

>   By all accounts,
>   (and there is only one):

Eye-Witness:
    'The signore
    was leaning over the side, apparently
    coughing out his insides into a
    passing gondola.
    I took him to be
    the usual Luftwaffe delegate lagering
    the lagoon,
    surrounded by his friends,
    all bellowing in unison.

    'And did not feel obliged
    to alert the commanding Blueshirt
    (after all it was a diretto,
    and I have a family to go to…).[1]

    'I presumed the party were on their way to
    the Palazzo Labia (closed at this time and
    in any case in restauro).

    'And turned my attention to the D'Annunzio plaque in
    the Wagner Gardens:

'In questo palagio	'In this palace
L'ultim a spiro	the soul hears
Odono le anime	the last breath
Perpetuarsi che	perpetuate itself like
Lamb i marmi'.	the tidal wash on the
	marble walls'.

    "It reminded me of the war.'

        BANGE STIMMUNG!

    'Passing San Geremia
    it struck me (vague fears)
    that somewhere between
    Fondaco dei Turchi

and the Scalzi,
something had happened

'which could only be explained
by interpreting Jacopo Robusti's many canvasses
depicting St Mark's body being snatched
from the Infidels by Venetian merchants
as TRUE TO LIFE.[2]

'For between stops,
the delegate and his cortege
had vanished from sight,

'like Tiepolo putti
on a damp ceiling
dissolved in a drip.

'Si!
TRIONFO DELLA MORTE,
LA MORT DE VENISE.'

When death strikes our shadows become
accusing wraiths, and can't be tamed
through parlour games by Nodes & Son,
or family plots, or self-contained
boxing in the columbarium.
Dust to dust is not fair exchange.
What's in between's been robbed in sum.
Replaced for all time by the strange
unearthed photo of the loved one,
touched up in tempera, and framed.

Interpol:
        An utterly examined death is
        unbelievable.
        Still,
        facts can be met
        halfway.

Pressman:
> The head line
> has a deadline.

Interpol:
> Dead man in the lagoon.

Pressman :
> DEAD MAN IN THE LAGOON
>   – doing fine

Editor:
> You don't arrive at the truth.
> You arrive with it.

Reuters:
> All the angels in architecture
> with their winged weltanschauungs
> can't deliver such buttresses.

Editor:
> Our pleasure is, not to be proved right,
> But NOT to be proved wrong.

All:
> There is no point
> in holding your finger
> up to the wind:
>
> the spittle
> may not dry
> on the side
> you want.

Hugh's footsteps made a hollow sound
because no one was in his shoes;
and ghost footprints upon the ground
lead nowhere; and for want of clues,
his phantom shade was free, not bound

by contracts, and gave interviews.
'Our hero sleeps in other's dreams'.
'Who sleeps in his?' 'No one, it seems'.

CODA

Behind San Rocco
on the Calle Tintor,
a whisper is heard
from a derelict palace,
'Is graffiti an Italian word?'

Tourists!
        High flamingo bodies,
        goldfish complexions,
        stuffed in Van der Rohe
        airports, art-galleries,
        4th World refugees
        flicker by in a strobe.
        There they go, tallyho,
        over the glaucous globe,
        missing their connections,
        and their families.

Trapped
by a freak storm,
wrapped
in pink plastic
        (sold
at the drop
of a thunderbolt
on San Marco)
on their way to
Fondamenta dei Mori.

The shoots
of Venice are a shanty town
of private
          niagaras.

The downpour
will end in a

THUNDERFLASH:

Wall LIT
UP,

BRAVI I MORTI,
BRAVI I MORTI

(Is graffiti
an Italian word?).[3]

CANTO TEN

> 'I dealt him two blows
> for at the first he fell dead'.
> – Bevenuto Cellini

Nowhere is safe as a hotel.
A mumbled name, a numbered key.
All human contact by a bell,
and breakfast in your room is homely.
Who's out, who's in? Who is to tell?
The only danger is the lonely
lounger who slopes around the place
spotting labels on the suitcase.

Doc McGuiness had a penchant
for tourist traps, and would not stay
where the guidebook gives a mention
(guest-books to sign, and desk delay);
trap managements are straight henchmen;
the chambermaids are changed each day;
the mirrored walls have seen it all—
slow suicides, the early call…

Sleek shacks beside an aerodrome,
or motorway, or red-light spot,
he likes: where glass will vie with chrome;
and dogs and cheques and wives are not
encouraged; here you hear the moan
of heavy traffic as you drop
off to bad dreams, or dry-dive
death: Hotels Othello or Odette.

Or dives called Daemos near stations,
with peeling fronts and dark name-sign.
The padrone and relations
sit in the lobby, raking crime.

Clients aren't welcome invasions.
A boy checks you in, in double-time,
and humps your baggage up five floors,
though rooms are empty in the lowers.

Doc chooses the opposite of home,
feels more secure with decor decked
for one night stands with no one known;
where passport papers are not checked;
a place some pimp might call his own:
the wire coat-hangers, nice neglect
by sullen staff who get the gist;
guests in this world need not exist.

Tonight (blinds down and open zips)
the CHI, Chioggia is Doc's doss.
Chioggia, choke on that, fat lips!
Doc doesn't, he's just killed his boss,
the grappa bottle that he grips
still hot from the speedboat across
the wildcat bay to lie-low land
where package tours are promised sand.

Albergo Chi is a prefab
fiasco in the Sotto style.
The architect made dozens, drab
but daring, while he made a pile.
These high-rise dinosaurs now sag
along Chioggia's golden mile;
but spring up straight for brochure snaps,
Walhallas destined to collapse.[4]

Midnight.
        Is Doc McGuiness bored or bilious?
        McGuiness is bilious but not bored.
        Arrived too late for the table d'hote.
        Kitchen staff were even out of spit:
        despite bribes, Doc had to make do with:

      Gnocchi (dry),
      Petta di Manzo (high),
      Polenta (moist),
      Dolce Bongo (off).
      And all washed down
      with Rosso 2
      (the local brown
      forensic brew).

  Doc McGuiness is bilious but not bored.
  A guest perhaps of negative feedback.

1 a.m.

    Doc doodles
    with cheroot and pad
    sitting on the john;

    swigs grappa
    oiled with Chi gin.

    Ups the blinds
    and puts the window
    on a slat;

    the porous damp of night desponges

      mothdust around
        the bottled-fetus lamp
          throwing shadows on
            a well-worn copy of
              Albert Speer's *War*
                as Business Man-
                agement

                (cover-down
                on a tidy bed);

The view a
blank wall

                    A bottle
                    thrown against it;

                              Not quite

a blank wall

                    Spills Chi gin
                    oiled with grappa.

                              Has he lost
                              his grip?

not quite
a blank wall:

                    dorsum of
                    another hotel,
                    the RHO[5]:

                              the latrine wing.

See through concrete a
parallelepipedon
of porticos
          squared off
in a hundred privy squats.
Each with an eye
          which lights up
                    when IN USE.

The latrine wing.

          The
     grandstand view
     in a twilight stadium
     where every split
     second a match is
     lit.

           But not
         conducive
                     to sleep.

Tootle
of a flute.
           A wind calls
         through the plumbing;

                     The ballcock
                     crows.

3 a.m.
           Doc spits phlegm
           into the waste deposit
           and imagines

                     (Chi gin &
                     grappa)

                           a woman

                     redesigned as
                     a water-closet:

Lights on and off in
the latrine wing.
O cisterns call:

         flush follows
         flicker, flicker
         follows flush.

Pits
his mind
back to something...

The blank wall
weeps excrement

> (flush follows
> flicker, flicker
> follows flush).

This is Sottomarina
(Chioggia's golden mile):

DAWN CHORUS.

4 a.m.
> Sleep is the interest paid
> on the capital of death.
> The higher the rate that's made,
> and if every night it's met,
> the longer the day's delayed
> for which redemption is set.

5 a.m
> As the grappa dark sea
> meets the Chi gin sky
> the latrine wing
>   flickers out,
> and Doc
> contemplates his blood
>   (indolamines low)
> and his lower brain stem
>   (the theta into his
>   hippocampus
>   won't go),
> and
> prays:
>   All ye in Mammoth Caves
>   Kentucky , synthesising waves
>   in brains deprived of sleep,
>   hear me on your hospital bleep:

Klitman and Dement,
Bollard, Block and Dews,
McGinty and Leconte,
Lucero, Black and Hughes,
Hennevin, Hardman, Dent,
Zimmerman, Toyva, Ponte,
and Gombosh, it is sleep I want
and not results that shake
the obvious until it yells,
'The more we stay awake
the less we are ourselves'.[6]

                 The telephone begins to sound.

              Dement! Dement! Is that Dement?
        Tell Gombosh to come round.
         Marshall the hardware through the vent...

"Baltasar[7] brings your early call,

                   20 peacocks,
            30 lions,
         40 camels,
       60 dogs,
      70 monkeys
and 80
                nothings at all'.

Doc doodles
with cheroot and pad
sitting on the john.
This litany has always meant
much more to him than mogadon...

The pencil squiggles a last graph.
Who says that sleep cannot be planned?
Pad closes on a helpless hand.
And dreams come to have the last laugh.

CANTO ELEVEN

> 'Trust no evidence
> not even your own'.
> – T.H. Huxley

DOC'S DREAM

A frozen monster
thaws on to the terrain
and the Laguna Vita
is a ball of water
inside Doc's brain.

        Float into the cranial cave
        on a tidal D-sleep wave,
        a frogman in grey matter;
        past dura and pia mater
        filigree'd in torn fronds;
        explore the cistern of the pons,
        and corpus callosum: the root
        of all evil, and cognate truth.

Cerebellum:
        How goes it there?

Two Gyri:
        All dead.

        Slip inside and feel Doc's theta
        bloated with Laguna Vita.
        θ: death warrants more than that sign
        for votaries of Zazen time[8]:

Not as usual looking at
the everyday shackled form
of a conquered monster, but
in untrammeled dreams seeing
things monstrous and free.

    Dreamtime in the frontal cortex:
    a goldfish in an open mouth,
    the flutter of an eye-lid;
    bits of ideas the brain collects
    in incubi exploding out
    the ideographs for the id.

All those things you think you did
splutter up and lava out
Goyana in a vortex:

        lobster-casing and chewed gum,
        gossamers and bange stimmung,
        syringes, swabs, biro-springs,
        and stray offal with tarred wings,
        teabags, toilet paper, plates,
        and blue torsos of inmates
        from La Grazia, San Clemente
        (sanctums for the round the bend)[9].

.... the eyelash ....
.... of the troubled mens ..
...... closes on this ....
.... goulash ...., ...
..... archipelago. ....
.... dream menu
or a recipe for madness ....
a Laguna Morta stew ....
.... or the bare bones
of it. ....

Cradle your catalepsy ....
and read the fossiled palm ....
wrinkling a route on ....
the inside of Doc's. ....
.... brainplate ....
Wave goodbye ....
to the Isola de Dolore ....
.... the story is going ....
somewhere .... AND WE'RE OFF:

    Per omnibus saecula saeculorum,
    snake-run from Venezia to Chi.
    O Ferrybus, would there were more of them.
    Still one is enough to get by.

    Omerta, it's manned by a fine crew
    of leopards, young, savage, 2-legs:
    one drives, and three watch, take a dim view
    of stopping to pick up wine-kegs;

    Blueshirts, dry clean as the blue skies, and
    languid as butchness allows
    (one wonders sometimes at the crew size
    like a ship with Three Graces as prow).

The passengers, mainly grass-widows,
weighed down with strawed parcels and brats.
Their menfolk won't notice their Mass clothes:
detenuti can only see hats.

What gifts do they lug to the prison for
their prodigal's solitary hours?
Fretsaws, it is hoped, must be hidden
in the lapfuls of cemetery flowers.

Conductor-pard:
>ALL ABOARD
>Metacarpus to
>Tarsus;
>
>next stop
>Patella.

>Wheel-pard checks moustache in the mirror.
>Starts up—hand brake on—the tyres scream.
>Grass-widows and parcels thrown nearer.
>The crew settle back, a low lean.

Wheel-pard:
>How goes it there?

Pards:
>All dead.

>A nonno won't lie down, waist naked,
>swings a brandy flask on to the aisle
>and dances a step. Will he make it,
>as his dentures death-rattle a smile.

Nuisance nanno:
> BRAVI I MORTI.

>> Grass-widows thrown down on their parcels
>> whisper, 'Basta, old man, we've got life!
>> For the sake of free fares, those arseholes
>> mustn't know that Dead Men have a wife'.

> BRAVI I VIVENTE

>> The bus tumble stops, all its ten tons.
>> And Wheel twists nonno's arm in a knot
>> as his pards close in like myrmidons
>> to put back the straight-jacket they've got.

Conductor-pard:
> Everybody out,
> everybody in,
> everybody in-
> side OUT.

Grass-widows:
> Grazie

Conductor-pard:
> Prego

>> A radabarbara
>> in a samarra
>> rises and blesses
>> the oenanthic air
>> with an aspergillic prayer,
>> waving sheafs
>> of raw spaghetti
>> over the cowering throng,
>> and
>> sprinkling sago confetti.[10]

        Nonno trussed, the bus screams off.
        Sergi Soukhoroutchekov,
        two-wheel Champion of the World,
        speeds past at the speed of sound.
        And the fungoidal sheep, hurled
        into Doc's lap, a nibble's found.
          AND DOC CAN'T WAKE UP

Per omnibus
saec. saec.,
the bus is stopped.

                At a graveyard.

Busload of mourners dig
in chains with spades
handed out by the pards.

                A mass grave.

Flagons of red wine
and baskets of fresh rolls
are laid in the plot.

                A pagan custom.

And earth is thrown in
until the death-hatch is
made whole.

                The status quo.

     The abandoned wives rake up the ashes
       and release the nonno, now sober.
         Must troup back, flashing their bus-passes.
        The Festivo Morte all over.

Wheel-pard:
>Maledetto!

Conductor-pard:
>How goes it there?

Wheel-pard:
>THE BUS IS DEAD.

Grass-widows:
>What's wrong, what's wrong?

Conductor-pard:
>The problem is the parts don't fit,
>and to replace them would cost
>more than the Company can muck
>together. It looks as though we're stuck.
>The Wheel-pard says we're truly lost.

Sober nonno:
>For how long?

Conductor-pard:
>>For all eternity
>>if necessary.

Grass-widows:
>Lost, lost, lost, lost
>etc. etc. (isterico).

>>The busload is a moiling mass
>>of sardined widows, seen through glass
>>by Doc, embossed on the bonnet.
>>Looking in, he wants to vomit,
>>seeing himself in Wheel-pard's seat
>>being flayed by hags with sides of meat,
>>while Blueshirts shuffle cards.
>>>Doc crawls

on to the bloodstained windscreen,
and bawls:

Keep calm, you idiots.

I have a MAP.

After a struggle with a senile sheep,
Doc uncaps his brain-plate
and takes out
a fossil
which he imprints on
the steamed up windscreen:

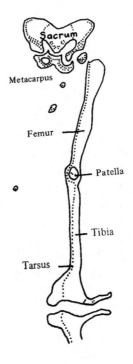

This is ridiculous

CANTO TWELVE

> 'A rude awakening'
> – Anon

Fleur:
    This is ridiculous!

Doc:
    Am I awake?

    A florid umbra hovers over Doc's Gyrgatus[11]
    It is a kimono cascading down a chocolate coiffure:
    Fata Morgana from the straits of Messina? No, Fleur,
    shoe in hand, hairpin in mouth, neck a praying mantis,
    throws herself on the neitherdown of a bad night sleep;
    prostrates herself before Doc's prostate in a flesh heap.

This is ridiculous.

    Daylight cuts segments on his face
    Fleur struggles with the shutters: they slat.
    McGuiness greets the dark with an embrace
    that buries himself in frumpy fat.
    A Rubens pietas them enlace.

    A squeezed sponge sops up the cataract.
    Rising with a belly button peck,
    Fleur lights a cheroot, matter of fact,
    and puts it in the teeth of the wreck
    whose treasure she must one day abstract.

    McGuiness laughs a little wooden laugh
    for the wall he feared is now, in lieu
    of ghosts, papered with his other half,
    whose designs are glaring. 'Just like you
    to come when I'm helplessly *paf*[12].

Fleur:
> The girls at Harry's are all talking about a severed leg washed up at the Papadopoli, miraculously still bleeding.

Doc:
> What about the rest of it?

Fleur:
> That's the strangest thing. No body was found.

Doc:
> Sharks, sharks, I suppose.

Fleur:
> But surely there aren't any sharks?

Doc:
> That's what you think.

Fleur:
> In the Lido too?

Doc:
> Count yourself lucky.

Fleur:
> What
>   happened
>   with
>   Hugh?

Doc: ...

Fleur:
>Mac, tell me something. Why did the sharks
>leave the leg?
>>Why don't they like legs?

Doc:
>Probably because they aren't sharks.
>>Fleur, turn a haunch:
>where is white lunch?

>>>(Agitation in flesh folds
>>>a tube of chocolates unrolls,
>>>each slab sealed.
>>>>Doc, nail surgeon,
>>>dissects the silver foil,
>>>>spills out some
>>>pulver. Touches and snorts.)

>>Pure as bleached bone.
>>>(So shares the beans with Fleur).
>>Brand-name Theobrome.

>A gossamer descends upon the pair,
>cocoons the couple in a frigidaire
>suspended spasm like a frozen fit.

>White Angel, sustain them in your vice-grip.

Fleur:
>How goes it there?

Doc:
>All dead.

CODA

      In the beginning was the bean.
      Theobroma the tree:
      ostrichlike evergreen,
         sprout and lower canopy.
Halfway up the mountainside,
Theobroma the tree.
Equatorial jungle-pride:
shades its flowery progeny

from snow cataracts in spring;
Theobroma the tree:
from sunflies cactuses will bring.
Bouquets of bean-pods grow free.

Inca women chew and spit
(Theobroma the tree)
into bean-pot, pound up with
Maize, Vanilla, Peony:

Xocoatyl, Cocoa-cake.
Theobroma the tree.
Probably an emetic.
Ancient Aztec recipe.

Cucu women use it too,
but with pulps of Lady leaf.
Starvelings find sniffing the brew
better than Oxfam Relief.

Sugar workers in Peru
chew it raw. While in New York
sophisticates known to Hugh
whiff it pure from tuning fork.

Cucu women's remedy—
cocaine mixed with cocoa chyme—
struck Hugh, not as démodé, rather
reason for a shrine.

He raised fiduciary loans,
and sunk all his private means
in Cioccolato's catacombs
to manufacture chocolate-beans…

NOTES: ACT TWO

[1] Blueshirt. Italian Transport official.

[2] Jacopo Robusti: Tintoretto

[3] "Bravi i morti". Praise be to the dead. (A fisherman's catch-cry, Venice.)

[4] CHI and RHO. Greek initials for Christ.

[5] 'All ye in Mammoth Caves'. Nat Klitman conducted seminal sleep-deprivation studies in Kentucky, USA, from the 1960's. Dement, Gombosh et al are coeval authors in the field.

[6] Baltasar Gracian. The litany of beasts is from Baltasar Gracian's *The Oracle*.

[7] Zazen. A yoga sweat worked up by thinking the worst.

[8] La Grazia and San Clemente. Islands in the lagoon, Venice, uninhabited except for an 'isolation hospital' for mental illness.

[9] Radabarbara. Full-blown mature woman.

[10] Samarra. An execution gown.

[11] Gyrgatus. A bed with a straight jacket.

[12] Paf. Plastered, drunk.

Act Three

"Life goes upwards in a spiral. If you study
the shadows of the past below, you can gauge
the uncertain curves ahead, and more surely judge
the gradual arch up which you climb."
– S. Kierkegaard

CANTO THIRTEEN

> "A voice as I draw closer seems to cry,
> 'Roll up, roll up, and see the victim
> die'."
> – Dante

Scene:
    A basement at the foothills of
    Cioccolato, a fortress town.

Dram. Pers:
    The Body Inside
    Vector (black student in exile)
    Velocity (his play-sister)

Vector:
    It could be Somewhere (Who's been here before?),
    but it is not. And neither is it Nowhere,
    or Nowhere That You Know, this shanty shed
    and mausoleum for the manque dead.

    A purgatorial place to sit on stash.
    Every mod. con., plus which a cooncan hand
    to while the time. The peaches are Bear Brand.
    Cool out the cachė: you can handle ash.

    No snatcher Sambo with a rainbow sash,
    half-stepping on the track of Lillygrand
    would find this hide. It's salamander sand.
    A basement window cluttered up with trash.

Body Inside:
    O hot and bothered day, for fatter flies.
    Swat misses them: distemper keeps its clean.
    The blood is sluggish as tomato-juice
    poured by a dipsomaniac. What gnat
    would feed on serum from sebaceous glands?

Under the armpits everything is sweat.
Even the gangrene is moist. A wet towel
hung overnight to dry still sops with hume.

Vector:
    'Waterboy, won't you bring the water round'.

Body Inside:
    Mosquitoes can't be choosers. They light on
    a phantom limb, the feeling still is there.
    But metastasis can't sustain a midge.
    The fever-fly smells blood, it scars the air.
    Blood blackened into dust by porous damp.
    Hold flight an instant. On antennae glide,
    lulling the host-to-be with muted Hmmmmm.
    As dressing loosens, swoop will find the stump.

Vector:
    'If you don' like your job, buddy, set your bucket
    down'[1].

Velocity:
    "When a man's sweat
        is strong enough
      to repel mosquitoes,
          boy, dat's character"[2].

        Look in, the stiff is jumping on the spit.

Vector:
    A bar-B-Q in hell, the devil's bit.

Velocity:
    Face as black as a bad night for Jim Crow.

Vector:
    A burst vein makes every man a negro.

Body Inside:
>The sun cuts diamonds in the saffron haze
>which fractures like mirages being found out.
>Each crack in it reflects the world, the same
>as spiders might, or molecules with specs…
>Window! Lookout! Squint eyeglass for Cyclops,
>capsuled in cement, flaying while it sets!
>The shadow of a shrimp, in perspex, pinks…

Vector:
>"Sugarland sisters' got a babysweet jellyroll.
>When dey walks dey reels, Lardy, rocks behind.
>Dat's enough to wake up a Dead Man's mind".

Body Inside:
>Body returns from coma. There is hope.
>One leg less, true; still what remains can fix
>a thought about mosquitoes that have missed:
>DESPAIR IMPROVES THE AIM. IT WILL TONIGHT.
>AND BLOOD WILL MARK THE WALL, will mark the
>wall…

Vector:
>Blood, did you hear? That means us, Soul,
>we're for the wall. That there pootboot
>wants Blood to waste in his manhole.
>Haul ass, play-sister, I would say, let's shoot.

VECTOR'S STORY

My momma dropped me on Manhattan Isle,
and I is black, but O my soul's high yella:
yoked like an Easter egg, true Tate & Lyle
plantation rape-child, Harlem whatdehella.

My ruined mother taught me how to pee
while sitting down at welfare conferences.
And how to cross an 'i' and dot a 't'
while writing on the walls my confidences.

She taught me how to run down lines, talk trash;
to climb forbidden hoists, and cat a pad;
to bogart homeboys: shark silt-bone, dress flash;
rap, sass, mack, ass, cop, hop, lowride a Cad
    (wid four doors and four whores,
    a zoot in the suit,
    their pimp in the booth.
    I's real bad, I's REAL BAD).

The summas of my schooling were all Long Hot.
The Paradise Teenbar: kelt, skag & juice,
and sidewalk boogaloos; this ignite spot
for Whiteys to turn pink with bugaboos.

The Videots stay tuned, 'A Full-Scale Riot';
J. Edgar on TV; the Racer's siren,
Black Youths set the Lincoln Centre alight.
3 Bs… the ghett-o jumps… Burn Baby Burn.
    (Because a situation
    is stupid does not mean
    it is simple).

In Noland High School, Baby Brother goofs
with sheath machines, and fixes waterbombs;
and lindyhops across the Project roofs,
his pea-gun cocked to blow-off the condoms.

'The Sniper'! Spied by Sergeant Stretta, ex-
Cleanup Cop, suspended pending trial
for putting pressure on set-up suspects,
and out to prove his innocence. With rifle.

This One-man Ku Klux of Redneck romance
covered by curfew, starts the Backlash whites.
Trigger is Law & Order. Nervous hands.
A goophus spade is jigging in his sights.

Sarg hears the voices, 'Our white wives and kith
aren't safe from shines with peepers like pinballs;
their freelance lust leaves nowhere left to spit:
slave Samba free in subways for blonde spoils'.

How often has he heard it from The Man,
'Niggas is powers of darkness incarnate.
Since chains have slipped, now only bullets can…'
Rage picks a groin-shot and hits its target.

In sum my jive-ass Brother is a scape.
And Stretta hoops himself with a high five.
A Newsreel team were right behind his nape.
So Baby's execution was shot live.

> ("Un color bruno
> che non e nero
> ancora e 'l blanco
> more")[3].

SO

Street Blood Whitewashed,
all the hip hot boon coons
of goofs seen chilled on TV
were lifted to somewhere SAFE.

Two lamebrains were homberg'd
to Cioccolato's
College for Strangers.
And one of them is me.

Velocity :

>   And
>   what a place!
>   To base the case—
>   this square for triggers:
>   choc full of Mission'ry Niggas
>   eyes bigger than their stomachs
>   hully lump ducks in taffy frocks
>   ruining cobbles with off-the-cob boots:
>   Bungocongos hollering like deaf mutes
>   Shock hair like fifty thousand ants raising fists:
>   hot breakfasts for Balubas saved by Catechists—
>   BROTHER STUDENTS?

Vector:

> Enough to scare the pants off Garvey freaks.
> Pretender princes! Missionhut mistakes!
> Pretenders sport a Burton suit disguise
> and clutch their vinyl briefcase for dear lives;
> sheltering from *d'etats*, they wait a *coup*,
> scared white of course. White Fathers crossed with Kru
> are the Mistakes, a mongrel holy show
> (whatever God, Nyessoa can't say NO)[4]
> These miscegenes in jumble-sale first buys
> will propagate the Faith with whiter wives.
> Harambee the hymn, tamu the tune,
> Black Baby's future now is octoroon.
>
> All oofus donks converted into fades,
> and worse than white, they're runny rectrospades,
> who came for EuroPeonage, a cram course
> in Cioccolato Summa School; explores
> the power and knowhow of Renaissance Man,
> a realty to bring back to Abidjan;
> Dip. Phil. is hoodoo with a modern ring,
> and Machiavelli's patent medicine…
>
> No wonder Sis and me take dark detours:
> it's safe sightseeing in the open sewers.

Velocity:
> Brother, what's the bootsnatch
> on mosquito man?

Vector:
> Ritual waste job:
> the hack-work, I figures,
> of Mission'ry niggas.

Body Inside:
> The lower depths of town lie low.
> LowLife is dead. Slum clearance? No.
> Shattered streetlamps. No one about.
> A red-light district that's blacked out.
>
> What happened to vice? Gone underground?
> Or in a High-rise has it found
> a home-life squat? Anyone's guess.
> The wailing walls are tarred with a 'Yes
>
> to Abortion, Bravi I Morti,
> Woman's Life Begins At Forty,
> Legalise Mary, Free the Marthas,
> Lazarus Lives, Vote for the Party,
>
> Aldo Moro, Give God A Go......
> All adds up to a totem NO.
> Lower Hades's desperate data.
> Does Luigi still Love Renata?
>
> The lower depths of town lie low.
> Organised crime has gone skidrow.
> The Nu-Nite Enterprises wilt,
> flaked signs & symptoms of real filth.
>
> Namesigns of cover-joints and clips
> outlive their lure like fish & chips
> in garbage cans, or tomb inscriptions,
> or epitaphs after evictions.

Nominal simulacrums stand
in what's become down town deadland,
Bespoke Tailors, Taxidermists,
Dental Mechanics, & Hair Permists…

And so on. In this dust museum
the Hockshop's home. No human being
with sense or sentiment or shame
would come to pawn here: no reclaim.

Once thoroughfare, High Street of Sin,
the gay-dog's haunt, the schoolboy's dream.
Hallucinate all connoisseurs
of LowLife, and memory masseurs.

Gone is the Paradise of Pards,
punk cadamites with printed cards;
the Painted Whores of Babylon
to other porno pastures gone.

The whole kasbah is ghost refuse.
Fried to a char the Golden Goose.
All gone to the wall and ashes.
Above an Autostrada passes…

And I must lie in this basement,
dead to the world, but gaining strength.

CANTO FOURTEEN

> "A man's character
> can only be judged
> after he is dead"
> – Count Vittorio Alfieri

Scene:
    The towertop plateau of Cioccolato

Dram. Pers:
    Living statue of Dante (bronze)
    V&V (sitting at his feet)

Statue:
    O Cioccolato,
Who would have thought you'd stoop so low,
City of the corrugated plain!
Your patron saint, St Ubad, prayed in vain:
once fortress town for brigands to recoup;
rogues like Respanti, and Fortebraccio,
sojourned within your territorial poop.

I, Dante Alighieri, spent some time here,
Vo poetizzando, and in hiding from
Black Ghibellines, and patron Malaspina.
Now I'm a landmark for the tourist throng,
outside a gabinetto always shut,
cursed as an inconvenience, and defiled.
Around my pedestal, a rubbish glut;
while once a year the goliards run wild,
and hang a laurel-wreath upon my nose;
that's on St Hubert's feast-day[5]: the ingrates
deface the verse inscription with low prose,
and crown my poet's brow with paper-plates.

Throw snowballs at the sun: they harm it not.

My desecrated statue is floodlit,
a festival of light in apricot
reveals the 'cosmic clown' of their crude wit,
a laughing stock to every empty mind,
like Can Grande's fool[6] who piled my plate with bones.
'Dogs eat their bones, but I leave mine behind'.
I answered thus, and left them for my poems.

O Cioccolato town, you once were proud
to hold a hermit Pope within your bounds;
still Benedict the Ninth left in a shroud;
poisoned by figs, fresh from the convent grounds,
served by an altarboy dressed as a nun.
A Roman plot that undermined your great
and ancient reputation for Asylum;
endangered Popes and princes spurned your gate:

O Cioccolato town, now famed for chocolate!

Vector/Velocity:
    According to the guidebook
                        REAL BAD ONCE
    Place to cool off fly jives
                        REAL BAD ONCE
    Now creep round the nite-dives
                        O LORDY LORD
    Discotheque Belacqua
                        REAL BAD ONCE
    Limps with lame Brubeck
                        REAL BAD ONCE
    Not a jump with neon
                        O LORDY LORD

    City of the plain
    digestive chocolate.

Dante:
> Un color bruno
> che non e nero
> ancora e il
> > bianco
> > more.

Vector/Velocity:
> > Six long months I's been in this pen
> > > Yeah Yeah YEAH YEAH
> > Don't want a come to this place again
> > > Yeah Yeah YEAH YEAH
> > Don't worry, Buddy, I ain't corning back
> > > Yeah Yeah YEAH YEAH
> > Don't want no fine clothes and no Cadillac
> > > DROP 'EM DOWN
>
> > Drop 'em down the drain.
>
> > Statue,
> > you're the Main
> > Square Man,
> > of Bam gam—
> > bitabrainfame
> > What do
> > you make of it?
> > Spit.

Dante:
> Una lunga leggere presto …leopards!
> I saw you—as a student in Bologna—
> rag the popolo grasso like true goliards.
> I'd have cut my beard and Bruno[7] to have known you.
> Lucus a non lucenda,[8] behind blinds
> in my solinga camera, lisping numbers.
> Your minstrel motley, and dolphin-like good times,
> mocked all I stood for, and still disturb my slumbers.

> Today I meet you like snow touched by the sun.
> You melt even the rock buried beneath the snow.
> You who are as God intended, free in tongue
> and divers pentecostal drives which know not NO…

Vector:
    Thanks.

Dante:
    Prego.

Velocity :
                Poppastoppa,
    you get the Poet's Banana.
    Give it to him, brother.

Vector:
    I done-a warn you, sister,
        Birdland Bronze is no cool cat:
    dude's like a gorilla
        in a laundromat.
                HE'LL EAT THE STUFF.

Velocity:
    You better jump in a hurry
    or Bronze will start to shoot more lines.

Dante:
    What is this he gives me, Little Sister,
    what gift from youth to age? May I unrap?
    The silver foil is thunder in my hands.

Vector:
    Better read the health warning
    on the righteous wrapper:
        'Dr Erlenmeyer, personal communication:
    has a limited use in medicine as a local
    anaesthetic. More addictive than morphine,

it has been called the third scourge
of humanity'.

Dante:

                O octogone
          gift, inside your cone
         would seem to be a demon.

Velocity:

          'Dr C. Koller, Wiener Wochenscrift:
makes you feel as though you had a good dinner,
and you don't need to bother about anything…
Can cure diabetes. And break a heroin habit. Non-addictive'.

Dante:

          The sun has a shadow in its gizzard.
          It dances in the eyes of a lizard…

Vector:

Look here, D.A.,
        ain't you seen snow before?
Sister, half the stuff
        is spilling on the floor.

Velocity:

Poppastoppa,
swallow your booger,
don't breath a word
except in.

      (A stripped banana
      left in the air
      goes black, an'
      dat is bad).

>   Stuff's a rose.
>   Put is to your nose
>   and sniff the pollen
>   from the bloom.
>   There goes.

Dante:
    O milky mauve,
      O brio,
         O flair.
    O purigo!

Vector:
    Sister, its time to join this molten Bronze

>   at home
>   on the Rio
>   Grand
>   with namebrand
>   Theobrome.

CANTO FIFTEEN

> "The greatness of Dante is
> in Lamarck's backward descent
> down the ladder of living
> creatures: the lower forms
> of life are the hell of humanity".
> – O. Mandelstam

Scene:
    The same

Enter:
    Fleur and Doc (as tourists)

Fleur:
    The scenic heights!
              Is this the view?

Doc:
    It's what is called a vantage point.
    The mountains beyond are eight deep:
    can't count then tonight for the mist.
    Out there, could you see, each star is
    an open nerve ending to
    everything you should want...

Fleur:
    Not sure I like the company.

Doc:
    Madame, avert your eyes, for we
    stand on the edge of a frontier
    that knows no bounds.
                  Those lollards haunt
    the long cut snows of yesteryear,
    squatting by statues! Let them sleep.

Fleur:
    In the arms of morphine.

Doc:
    With their eyes open for more.

Dante:
    How like a slug waking from sleep am I.
    Where is my shell? What flesh is this? Newborn…

Vector:
    Don't flake on us, D.A.

Velocity:
                   Bronze has turned green
    like a movie monster.

              This isn't his scene.

Dante:
    These early cobwebs hold me spellbound still…

Vector:
    Come back, an' hold your high. Man, make it last.
    This stuff is snow in summer.

Dante:
                   What having climbed
    more styloid steps than an old socle should,
    and sampled your potpourri, my heart breaks
    into capillaries, as though I'd slept
    in a nettle-bed and woken with scorpions.

Vector:
    Just a touch of bombox, swollen shot
    in your varicose, nothing serious.
    White Angel
        is sometimes
            over generous…

Dante:
>
> Trumpet a glory tocsin, the numbness fades.
> And I, Dante Alighieri, shake off this chain-mail.
> New life given to me, I rise on winged saliva.
> My chrysalis is a thousand tapestries
> with sunrise patterns, an eyeball around me.
> 0 weary limbs, wombed for centuries in stasis,
> unfurl like an inner ear. I can hear a strummm…

Velocity:
> Like when the grass is friendly
> and the night is white, huh!

Dante:
> I hear grass growing, and see crepuscular starlight
> piercing the heavens, and raining sparkles on me…

Vector:
> D.A. , you're on your way back. Keep coming.

Dante:
> I am the eye
> in a storm-cloud about to break.
> And I see a meteorite
> falling into the rising sun,
>
> and behold,
> a great movement of the earth
> and a white angel decends
> and rolls back the stone.
>
> All this happening on high.
> And I see a man passing by.
> And a great wind comes with him
> which makes a sepulchre of mountains,
> a whited sepulchre.
> And the rocks split into flints.
> And the flints conflagrate the foothills
> And the plains

        are no longer boundless,
      as they recreate themselves
      as meadows of red earth
        turning inside out,
  and swallowing all living creatures
and replacing them with giant cactuses…

  And I am
        very near
        discovering
              the secret of
              the PRIMAL-PLANT[9].

Doc:
    It flourishes
        in the dark arbour
  of your verses.

    SPROUT!

Dante:
        The Primal-Plant's found wanting here below.
        I could have acknowledged sassafras,
        cinnamon, and laurel, and couch-grass,
        myrtle, mountain-ash, and the murk-rose.
        But I did not.
        The Primal Plant grows
        not by seeding like magnolia,
        or reverie like Homer's moly,
        but through Inner Truth and Necessity.
        What ought to exist brought into being…

Doc:
  What about the Primal-Animal?

Dante:
> Remove the retinas from sleeping
> butterflies and you will find they weep
> for lost primacy, what might have been,
> which by default came to near nothing,
> and exists now only in sleep,
> and, within that, only in a dream…

Doc:
> What about the Primal-Fossil?

Dante:
> Profusions of God's creatures blasted by the sun
> and the movement of mountains,
>
> flung together for shelter, petrified for perpetuity,
> skeleton on skeleton,
>
> skeleton on skeleton, a pavement of interlocking
> bone
> crushed to a mere lick
>
>> of bone braccia:
>> a finger of sediment
>> in a cave niche…
>
> The earth spins slower at the thought of it.

Cioccolato stands on shifting soil.
Under its foundations, in catacombs,
homuncular hives in incessant toil
churn out the software source of Theobromes,
                        das liebe ding.

Leg gone…
          Live still…
                    Hugh crawls on blood, his own.
Blood clotted like a
                tortoise in the dirt.
His heartbeats boostered by the throbbing earth.
A manhole opens at his head: Hugh's home:
      a Tiepolo ceiling upside down
      reflects a man-made maze of stalactites
      contorted in concave. This grotto sites
      a factory in full flow beneath the town.
      Pothole putti, in shifts eternal, slave
      to fire this foundry in the lower depths.
      Mud-gravel rattles through the plant's pipettes.
      And blasted by life's blood it finds its grave.

    0 nugget nut,

the perfect product of Tsunami swamps,
nut of Cockaigne, riped in groves immortelle,

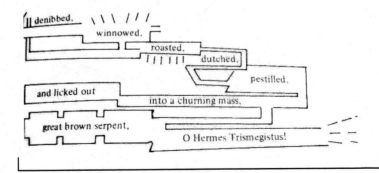

                    And alchemy's achieved: the slime stream golds
                    The bullion bars slab into coffined moulds.

                    And Hugo glories,
        'O churning moil…
                                    O everlasting confection…
        Puts the salami on the bread for myriad mouths.
                            Children of Cioccolato be grateful
                                    for this subterranean source,
                                            this manna,
                                                this mine.'
                    And stands on one leg, leaning on a rod,
                        divining power, an industrial god.

            The luceroles are alert as catfish.
            Stray dogs are barking madly at freak street fogs.
            The birds have vanished into double-rainbows.
            The moon tonight is full: there's triggers in the air.
            And blessed damozels
                            on balconies
                                    practise their
                                            Richter scales.

Doc:
            My head is clear.
                        We have killed time
        enough up here.
                        Now the down climb.

                                    (Exeunt omnes)

CANTO SIXTEEN

"If the mountain helps the weak it is not deliberate"
— A. Michaux

The Towertop plateau the city spirals
of
in snakes
a & ladders,
Piranesi down

stairways,
and balustrades bounding piazzas

widening the
as nude
descends,
until a stranger's
squarely amongst real people and rough granite
(as though Cioccolato
was a wedding cake

based on a pedestal of rock buns).
Here
steps
are missing
and railings
have been scrapped, defunct
funicular
plunges
to sand-pits,
the sedimental tufa-bed for the sewer

which sluices from the citadel to
the
bowels.

> O earth, slow
> slippage,   and the
>   and the creeping stops.

Vector:
> What's that there smoking behind the pilasters?
> Stinks like a Neapolitan nappy supper.
> Don't seem natural to me.

Velocity:
> Brother, it's sulphur.

Vector:
> Cheshire cat cigars wafting after dinner.

Velocity:
> Listen, I's don't like the smell of this precinct.
> The parallelepipeds have exhaust pipes
> coughing out assorted miasmas in clouds.

Vector:
> It's riot-police in Birnam smoke disguise.

Fleur:
> What about that NO SMOKE sign. Nothing's sacred.

Doc:
> It could be little businesses cropping up:
> Puff Packaging, an alternative product—
> Roll Your Own Fumeroles!

Fleur:
> O those poor puffs.
> Don't think they're going to make it if you blow them.

Velocity:
> Never did have a happy birthday. Here goes.

Fleur:
>Black girl, you are a genius. You've blown it out
>and into bubbles, oily rainbow ones too,
>and all the colours of a season in hell...

Doc:
>Out, out, brief frothing fumeroles, fill the air
>with your good bye glitter.

Fleur:
>   Really hip the way
>sulphur can change into soap in the right mouth.

Velocity:
>Some of them swell as they rise, but can't carry
>their size, and burst.
>   What do you make of them, Bronze?

Dante:
>In each sulphurous cloud there's a thousand flowers.
>In each pellucid flower, an apparition
>of White Lady cloaked in green holding a flame...

Doc:
>Wallpaper design for the Heavenly Mansion.

Vector:
>Or hippie version of the Blessed Virgin
>mass-produced in the moment of Assumption,
>all on the wings of pre-recorded mantras.

Doc:
>Fleur, set up a counter chant.

Fleur:
>   Hurry on the
>Boss is waiting. Hurry on the Boss is wait
>ing. Hurry on the Boss is waiting. Hur...

Vector:
>Doc, the ground! Just like the Apollo before sawdust is thrown down for whitehot devil dance. I can't stand it.

Doc:
>Just like Furey's frying pan[10] you could skewer a ballerina on it. Still, we gotta take risks with plastic soles if we're to get to the bottom of this. Dante, lead on.

Dante:
>Let he who names the place not rest content.[11]

CANTO SEVENTEEN

> "Das Urorganismus (or Primal-Plant)
> possesses within itself
> to take on manifold forms, and,
> at any given moment, ocean-like,
> it assumes the form most suited
> to the environing conditions,
> the circumstantial world."
> – Goethe

Doc:
    Roll
    back the stone from the manhole.
    Hugh's down there. I smell his brain.
    Vector, let down the winch chain.

Vector:
    Boss, why sweat ourselves to raise
    this Lazarus, dead four days.
    You get his stink?

Fleur:
        He stunk in life.
    Black boy, ready with your knife.

Velocity:
    Cool it, brother, the earth's crust
    is cracking up. Get in first.

Fleur:
    The pot boils for him or you.
    Who's the lobster for the stew?

Dante:
    The earth's mantle's had enough
    of this cloak and dagger stuff.

> A cloud blurps from the manhole's mouth.
> And throws the rescue party down.
> A helpless heap of human moil.
> The earth moves with a slurping sound.
> Like when a plunger plumbing oil
> hits a ghost metro and spurts out
> the evening rush from underground.
> An earthquake is eructing
> Hugh at a seismic 6.2.

Fleur:
    Chuck a rock, boy, down that pit.
    See if he's alive.

Velocity:
    Just spit!

> How know a cry of rage from pain?
> Pain is profound, a tendering of tone:
> rage tells the truth, a loss of all control.
> Both rage and pain now echo in the hole,
> and fear, a blister, bubbles up the drain
> to blow the mouth, a trumpet of the soul
> that sounds no note of pity. All the same
> by muted shriek and basso moan, it's known
> the beast below is human and not tame.
> And in this dwarf basilica, Hugo's dome
> comes to a head that bursts through the membrane.

Velocity:
    A live-birth. And headfirst too.
    Dirty black, Messiah Hugh.
    Brother, shake out your switch-blade.
    Cut the cord. It's been okayed.
    White is black, and black is white:
     King of Spades is born tonight.

Vector:
> More second birth dat death brings
> for spiritual cops and cretins!

Fleur:
> See, his totem torso's jammed
> like a boiled egg in a cup.
> Cut his top off or he'll up
> and hatch all hell.

Vector:
>   Sister, take
> yourself a commercial break.
>
> Hole's the tube, and Hugh's the paste
> all squeezed out now to the waist.

Velocity:
> Yeah, white is black, and black's white:
> King of Spades will come out right.

Vector:
> No, egghead's a disaster,
> a fading telecaster,
> with a news-flash for Dead Man.
> I'll switch him off.

Velocity:
>   NO!

Hugo:
>   I am.
>   I am
>   the epicentre
> and this Corsican trap is my expression of it.
> Observe the fumes, the flow, the deep undercurrent.
> Beneath bubbles the ferment, the source, the molten coin.
> I sprinkle it with the hyssop of pure white, untainted.
> I bless this world and my confection.

I bless this font, this spring, this mountain stream, this mature river.
I bless this true solution.
Let it be harnessed to bring peace. Let it be harnessed to bring power.
This Primal-Plant
    surging with
        Inner Truth & Necessity
          is mine.
O Mother Earth's aborted child, Raumoku, Raumoku,[12]
deliver me, immured down here, Raumoku , Raumoku.

    I feel the universal joint
    locking the loose foundations,
    and the landmass jerk back into place.
    Erratic boulders paw the ground
    and await your sacrament.

    Loosen the bowels of the earth,
    Raumoko, Raumoko.
    Let there be excrement.

Doc:
    Tickle his throat, make him laugh.
    We'll split his body, half and half.

Vector:
    And pool his organs. Cool, right!
    Pulley him up to my height.
    Syringe, chainsaw!
        Where's the leg?
    Thigh rounded off like an egg?
    Lost left leg, you're a legend.

Doc:
    Or a cop's exhibit, friend.

    Sound one needs a shave.
        Nurse Fleur,
    scalp the right limb for the skewer.

> Prepare the body of Hugh
> for sacrifice by this Kru-
> trained specialist in the art
> of cutting.
>
> Ripper, let's start.

Vector:
> I'm a snow-surgeon. Yeti
> here's my specimen. Bet he's
> grateful for my chainsaw craft.
> Can keep alive what is halved.

Doc:
> Nice cut, kid. What viscera?
> Stuff them back. Straight misery
> isn't our aim. Kick start his heart.
> What we want is a mindful part:
> Hugo's brain taken alive.
> You will need your laser knife.

Fleur:
> A clean job.
> But why has
> everything gone silent?

Velocity:
> I hear nothing.

Dante:
> You will, but it will be too late.

Velocity:
> oooooooooh**hhhh**hhhhhhhhh

> A seismic shudder, and Hugo's free
> to come clean. It's Richter 7.3.
> He hangs suspended from the hoist
> above the moraine of the fault-line,
> now a tundra of tessellation, …

Doc:
>   OK, son,
> play your blades right, and don't waste
> the patient. Shoot straight beams, cut chaste
> incisions around the brainpan.
> That's the boy. The marzipan
> sack of mind matter inside
> is the Primal-Stuff, Pure White.
> Suck off the cannibal juice
> & squeeze-tease Hugh's brain-bag loose
> in one piece.
>
> >   Watch out, it's ripe.
> > Plant it on this totem pipe.

Vector:
>   What's that?

Doc:
>   Get a move on.

Dante:
> Too late my sisters and brothers.
> Nine on the Richter Scale, amen.
> This one is a klimaturz.[13]
> > Sudden drop in temperature.
> > Advancing ice-caps.
> > >   What then...?

Fleur:
>   We'll freeze.

Velocity:
>   Preserve us.

Doc:
>   Incred-
>   ibly good for the op-
>   eration. Vector, don't stop.
>   Deep-freeze surgery? No bugs
>   or anesthetic gulugs…

> | Seismic waves quiff up the hills around. |
> | Artic sastrugi corrugate the ground. |

Dante:
>   Minus 25 Celsius.
>   Gloria in excelus

Velocity:
>   Deep cool.

Vector:
>   Brain's hoisted and trussed.
>   The totem pipe is headed.

Doc:
>   Winch down.
>   Behold the dreaded
>   Primal-Source,
>   The EPICENTRE.
>   Plug the siphon in.
>   Enter
>   the puff pipette.

Fleur:
>   It's ours.
>   So eternal cauliflowers
>   can sprout…

Velocity:
>
> Nothing to sniff at,
> Hugh's White Essence.
> I'll give it
> the blowtorch treatment, and we's
> will have cauliflower and cheese.

Vector:
> Sister, you've done gone
> ignited
> the crucible.

Fleur:
> Hugh's sprited…

> A jetser of pure heaven
> hits the air.

Velocity:
> Christ, it's clouding…

Vector:
> Everyone,
> put up your umbrellas. This Hugh
> is fixing to hail. Break the splays till you
> get the canopy concave. Like Doc.
> Gotta stash every falling rock
> not to waste the EPICENTRE.
> Cioccolato's falling down.
> Render
> to yourself this falling star.

Dante:
> And to Hugh the things that are…

          The sphlincter opens
                         and a surge
          of all that matters
                         and does not
          eructs en masse
                         a perfect purge.
          The Great White Source
                         throws up its clot.

          In outer space
                         the stars thrombose
          the cosmic dust
                         in solar squalls
          space plasma fills.
                         The embol grows
          destroying light
                         as it snowballs
          compounding all
                         in its matrix.
          So fossilised
                         all life will churn
          to Great White Rock.
          The final fix.
          The Great White Rock
                         of no return.

THE END

NOTES: ACT THREE

[1] "Waterboy won't you…" Refrain from an Afro-American prison work-song. *Wake Up Dead Man* (Harvard University Press, 1972).

[2] "When a man's sweat… character". Carl Rakosi, *Americana XXXI*, Ex Cranium Night (1975).

[3] Dante.
Roughly translates: what is neither black or white? Burning paper.

[4] Nyessoa. Supreme god of Kru tribed (West Africa) whose myriad spirits are capable of evil as well as good.
Garvey. Marcus Garvey was a Black activist who started a movement Back to Africa.

[5] St Hubert. The patron saint of hunters. Also venerated by Dante as *La Vita Nuova*.

[6] 'Can Grande'. Erratic patron of Dante (see *Inferno*, passim).

[7] Bruno. Brunetto Latini, Dante's beloved teacher in Bologna.

[8] "Lucus a non lucendo": roughly translates "Hiding my light under a bushel".

[9] 'The Primal-Plant'. Goethe to Frau Von Stein, June 8th 1787: '…Tell Herder I am near the secret of the reproduction and organisation of plants, and that it is the simplest you can imagine… Tell him I have discovered quite definitely and unmistakably where the germ lies hidden, that I already have a general conception of the rest, and that there are only a few points now to fix more precisely. My Primal-Plant (the archetype), will be the most extraordinary creation in the world, one that nature herself might envy me. With this model and the key to it, one can go on and on indefinitely inventing plants, which must be consistent: I mean plants which, even though they do not exist, might exist, not just picturesque and poetic

shadows, or semblances, but possessing the quality of Inner Truth & Necessity. The same law will be applicable to all other living things'.

10 "Furey's frying pan". The cause of the world's final conflagration. (Folk-tale, Cork, Ireland).

11 "Let he who names the place not rest content". Dante, *Paradiso*, Canto XI (line 52). Trans. D. Sayers.

12 Raumoku. Maori goddess of earthquakes.

13 Klimaturz. Climate mutation.